ISBN: 978-1-57424-356-7
SAN 683-8022

Cover by James Creative Group
All Illustrations by Susan Oliver

Copyright © 2017 CENTERSTREAM Publishing, LLC
P.O. Box 17878 - Anaheim Hills, CA 92817

www.centerstream-usa.com

All rights for publication and distribution are reserved.
No part of this book may be reproduced in any form or by any Electronic or mechanical means including information storage and retrieval systems without permission in writing from the publisher, except by reviewers who may quote brief passages in review.

"Every child (and adults like me too!) can relate to Kylie's insecurity about her trumpet playing. Whether it's a musical instrument, our outward appearance, our speech or accent, etc., all of us have something we think is not very good about ourselves. The author of this book shows how Kylie learned to overcome her fears through a patient teacher, loving friends, and a magic lady who comes right out of the TV! This is a glorious book full of life lessons for all of us."

– Ted Perlman, Producer, musician, Theologian

"With wit and humor and a touch of fantasy, Thornton Cline offers a motivating and delightful story for kids who play musical instruments--and even for those who don't. The practical lesson that is gently woven into the story can be applied to all areas of life."

– Crystal Bowman, award-winning children's author

The Amazing Incredible Shrinking Trumpet

Kylie was a quiet fifth-grade girl. She dreamed of playing the trumpet.

One day at school, the band teacher, Mr. Adrian was signing up students for the band. He played the flute, clarinet, trombone and trumpet for the students.

“I want to play the trumpet,” Kylie said.

Mr. Adrian agreed to let her play trumpet if her parents said yes.

Kylie couldn't wait to tell her parents. They signed her up and rented a shiny, new trumpet from the music store.

When Kylie got home, she opened her case and picked up her trumpet. She held it in her hands. Kylie blew into it, but couldn't get it to play.

Weeks passed, as Kylie practiced hard so that she could play the songs in Mr. Adrian's class.

"You play well, but I can't hear you. You need to blow harder and play louder," Mr. Adrian said.

"But I'm afraid others will say I'm not very good," Kylie said.

"Don't worry about them. Think about your own playing. Play like you mean it," Mr. Adrian said.

The next day, some of Kylie's friends came over to her house after school.

"We heard you play trumpet," Tori said.

Kylie was silent.

“Would you play us a song?” Olivia asked.

“I’m not very good,” Kylie replied.

“We want to hear you play. Come on Kylie, let’s hear you play,” Tori said.

Kylie thought for a few minutes about what her friends had said.

She opened her case and held her trumpet in her hands. Kylie was nervous, but finally played.

“You’re good, Kylie,” Olivia said.

Kylie was silent.

"You think so?" she asked.

"Yes, you play your trumpet really good. You just need to play louder so we can hear you," Tori said.

"I'm nervous playing for people," Kylie said.

"You should play more often. You're really good," Olivia said.

"Thank you," Kylie said softly.

Week after week, Kylie continued to improve on her trumpet, but she was too nervous to play in front of people. And when she did, she played so softly that no one could hear her.

One night when she was about to fall asleep, she forgot to turn off her TV. She had been watching a music show.

Before she fell asleep, her eyes caught an amazing woman trumpet player with a band. Her playing was so good that it woke Kylie up.

"Wow, you're awesome," Kylie shouted to the woman on the TV screen.

Before she could say another word, the woman stepped out of the TV screen and stood before Kylie in her room. Kylie's eyes opened wide.

"Thank you," the woman said with a smile.

"How did you do that?" Kylie asked.

"Do what?"

"Walk out of my TV and into my room?" she asked.

"It's magic. Don't be afraid."

"What do you want?" Kylie asked.

"I came here to help you. You are a good trumpet student and you practice. But you don't believe in yourself. You are afraid of what others think. You are nervous when you play in front of people. You've got to play louder and stronger," she said.

"But I'm afraid to," Kylie said.

"Afraid you're not good?"

"Yes."

"My dear Kylie, you are very good. Take it from me. Believe in yourself. If you keep on playing softly, not believing in yourself, your trumpet will shrink until it vanishes. You will no longer be able to play and that would be sad," she said.

Kylie listened.

"Believe in yourself, believe in yourself, believe in yourself..." The woman said as her voice faded and she disappeared.

Suddenly the TV screen went black. Kylie fell asleep.

The next day Kylie laughed and thought it was all a dream.

"Trumpets don't shrink," she said.

As the weeks passed, Kylie continued to play her trumpet softly and was afraid to play in front of people.

One day, she noticed her trumpet was getting smaller. Day after day, her trumpet became harder to play because it was shrinking. She was embarrassed.

"Look at Kylie's trumpet," a band student said.

"Kylie, what happened to your trumpet? It's a miniature," Mr. Adrian said.

Kylie didn't say anything. She knew she had to do something quickly.

Maybe that woman from the TV was right, Kylie thought.

"Maybe I need to start believing in myself," Kylie said.

Kylie practiced a lot so that she could blow air into her trumpet and play louder.

"Believe in yourself," she told herself over and over again.

She looked into her bedroom mirror and told herself she was not afraid to play for people.

After a while, Kylie's trumpet started growing back to its full size.

She wasn't afraid or nervous to play for her friends, her parents or Mr. Adrian.

"You play so well and so loud," Mr. Adrian said.

"Keep up the good work. We can definitely hear you," her friends said.

Kylie became so confident on her trumpet that Mr. Adrian asked her to play a solo for the band concert.

That night, Kylie stood on stage and played her trumpet loudly. She played her solo perfectly.

The crowd cheered and applauded. They gave her a standing ovation.

Kylie smiled. It made her feel good. She finally believed in herself.

After the concert when the lights came on, Kylie looked around to find her parents.

Suddenly, she was surprised by someone she saw. Standing in the front row was the amazing woman who played trumpet on TV. The woman smiled and gave her two thumbs up. Then she disappeared.

Kylie's parents congratulated her.

"Wonderful solo, Kylie, we are proud of you," her mom and dad said.

"Thank you. I learned something about myself. I can't worry about what others think about my playing. I've got to believe in myself. And maybe one day I might be playing with a band on TV like my friend who visited me."

THE END

Song Titles

I Want to Play the Trumpet

Thornton Cline

Proudly ♩ = 108

F Gmin

I want to play the trum-pet, the shi - ny, shi - ny, trum-pet. The

3 Amin Bb/F F

one I've dreamed of play ing for so long______. Its loud and proud and sas - sy___.

6 Gmin Amin Bb/F C

Cla - ssi - cal and ja - zzy___. It's the ins - tru-ment made for me________. I

9 F Gmin C F

went to play the trum-pet, the shi - ny, shi - ny trum- pet________.

You Should Play More Often

Thornton Cline

Joyful ♩ = 102

C F C C G

You should play more of - ten__. You're rea - lly good. That's what my friend says.

4 F G C F C

Don't be ner- vous_, when you play your trum- pet__, play more of - ten.

7 F C/E Dmin G C F G C

You're real-ly good. You sound good. You should play more of- ten. You're rea-lly good.

Don't Worry What Others Think

Thornton Cline

Confidently ♩ = 110

C G C C

Don't wo - rry what o - thers think. Don't wo - rry what

4 G Amin F G F

o - thers say. All that mat-ters is you give your best when you

7 G Amin F G C

prac-tice and play___, don't be a - fraid___. Don't wo - rry what

10 G Amin F G Amin G C

o-thers think. Don't wo-rry what o-thers say, what they say.

Play It Like You Mean It

I Saw an Amazing Trumpet Player

Thornton Cline

She Jumped Right out of the TV

Thornton Cline

Surprised ♩ = 92

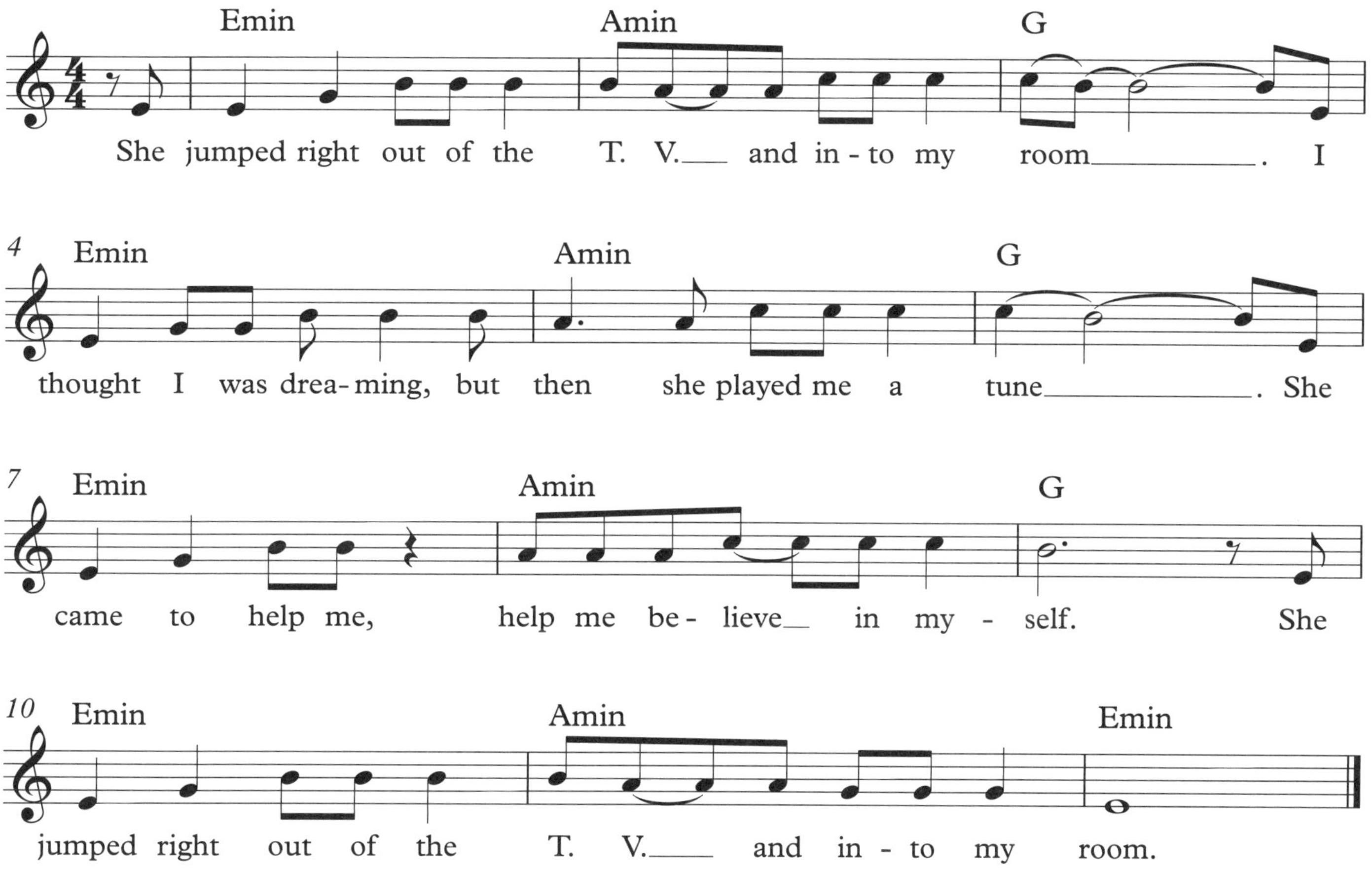

Emin Amin G

She jumped right out of the T. V.___ and in - to my room__________. I

4 Emin Amin G

thought I was drea- ming, but then she played me a tune__________. She

7 Emin Amin G

came to help me, help me be- lieve_ in my - self. She

10 Emin Amin Emin

jumped right out of the T. V.___ and in - to my room.

Believe in Yourself

Thornton Cline

With Confidence ♩ = 96

Trumpets Don't Shrink

Thornton Cline

Telling ♩ = 104

C F C
Trum-pets don't shrink. It was all a dream. The wo-man on T. V.

4 Dmin C/E F G
play - ing the trum - pet was all make be - lieve.

7 C F C
Trum-pets don't shrink It was all a dream, how she walked right out of that

10 Dmin G C F
T. V. Trum-pets don't shrink. It was all a dream.

13 F G C
It was all a dream.

What Happened to Your Trumpet?

Thornton Cline

Questioning ♩ = 96

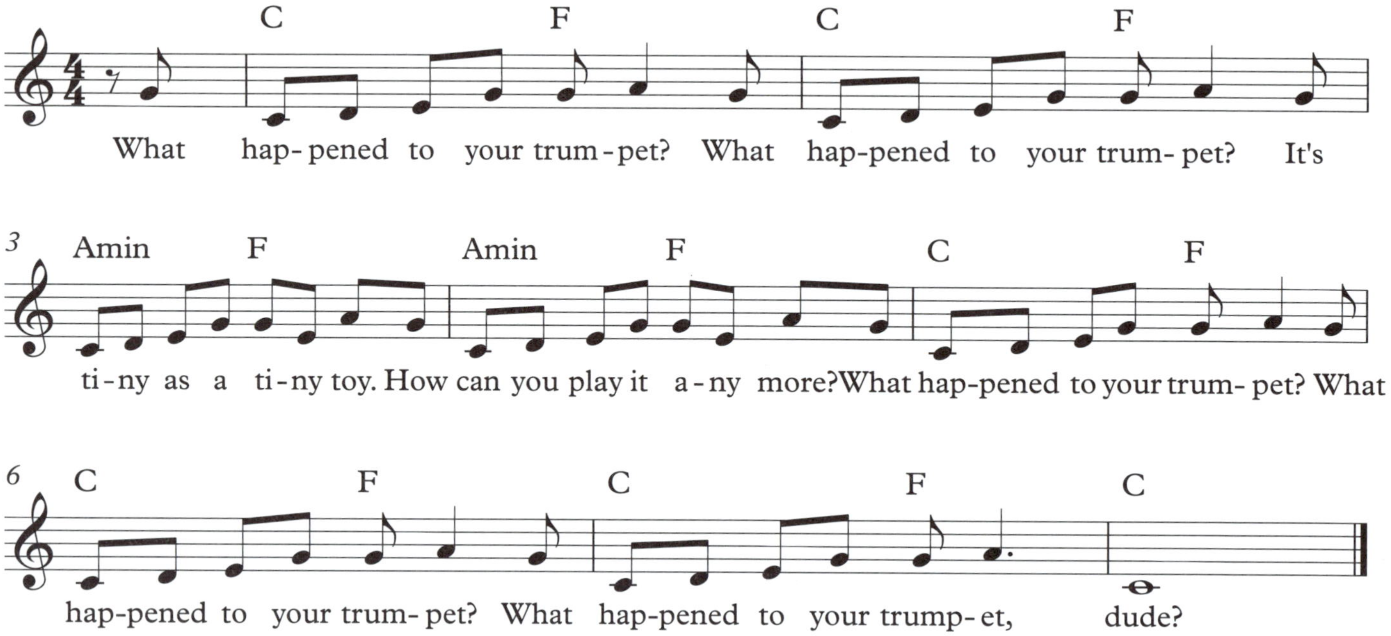

C F C F

What hap-pened to your trum-pet? What hap-pened to your trum-pet? It's

3 Amin F Amin F C F

ti-ny as a ti-ny toy. How can you play it a-ny more? What hap-pened to your trum-pet? What

6 C F C F C

hap-pened to your trum-pet? What hap-pened to your trump-et, dude?

My Trumpet's Back

Thornton Cline

With Confidence ♩ = 92

Biographies

Thornton Cline is author of fifteen books: *Band of Angels, Practice Personalities: What's Your Type? Practice Personalities for Adults, The Contrary, The Amazing Incredible Shrinking Violin, The Amazing Incredible Shrinking Piano, The Amazing Incredible Shrinking Guitar, The Amazing Musical Magical Plants, A Travesty of Justice, Not My Time to Go, The Amazing Incredible Shrinking Ukulele, Perfectly Precious Poolichious, El Increible sorprendente violin que se encogia, The Amazing Incredible Shrinking Drums* and Cline's ninth children's book, *The Amazing Incredible Shrinking Trumpet.* Thornton Cline has been honored with "Songwriter of the Year" twice in a row by the Tennessee Songwriter's Association for his hit song, "Love is the Reason," recorded by Engelbert Humperdinck and Gloria Gaynor. Cline has received Dove and Grammy Award nominations for his songs. Most recently, Cline has been honored with the Maxy Award for "Children's Book of the Year 2017". Thornton Cline is an in-demand author, teacher, speaker, clinician, performer and songwriter. He lives in Hendersonville, Tennessee with his wife, Audrey.

Susan Oliver is an award-winning songwriter and visual artist as well as illustrator. She is originally from Orono, Maine and attended the University of Maine as well as Portland School of Art. Known for her wide variety of styles, Susan has exhibited her artwork and also worked as a graphic designer. Her painting, "Moonlight Seals" gained national attention in efforts to raise funds for Marine Animal Lifeline, an organization dedicated to seal rescue and rehabilitation. Susan now resides outside of Nashville, Tennessee where she continues to write music and design art work for album covers for various musical artists, as well as illustrates children's books. *The Amazing Incredible Shrinking Trumpet* is Oliver's eighth children's book published as an illustrator.

Credits

Audrey

Alex Cline

Mollie Cline

God

Ron Middlebrook

Centerstream/Hal Leonard

Susan Oliver, illustrations

Crystal Bowman, editing

Elisabeth Jackson, editing

Mary Elizabeth Jackson, editing

Sumner Academy

Cumberland Arts Academy

Cumberland University

Marcelo Cataldo, transcriber

Hendersonville Christian Academy

Clinetel Music

Gallatin Creative Arts Center

Lawrence Boothby, photographer

Roberta Cline

Another Amazing Book!

“the perfect book for every young drummer...”
– Bart Robley

“This book teaches a lesson more valuable than any rudiment...”
– Chris Golden

THE AMAZING INCREDIBLE SHRINKING DRUMS

Story by Thornton Cline & Crystal Bowman, Illustrations by Susan Oliver

After begging his parents for drums, Matt receives a nice drum set and starts lessons with Mr. Thompson. Matt discovers he is talented. Playing drums comes easy for him. Matt brags to his friends on how good he is on drums. Matt brags so much that no one wants to be around him. One day, Matt visits a music store and watches a strange-looking man, dressed like a rock star, playing the drums. He is amazing. The man warns Matt that if he continues to brag, his drums will shrink until he won’t be able to play anymore. Matt discovers that it doesn’t pay to brag and learns how to keep his drums from shrinking. A songbook of 10 fun and catchy original tunes are included. (Recommended for ages 4-8).

00231633 .... $9.99

P.O. Box 17878 - Anaheim Hills, CA 92817

(714) 779-9390   www.centerstream-usa.com

More Amazing Books!

THE AMAZING INCREDIBLE SHRINKING VIOLIN
00142509 Book/CD Pack................................ $19.99

THE AMAZING INCREDIBLE SHRINKING PIANO
00149098 Book/CD Pack................................ $19.99

THE AMAZING, INCREDIBLE, SHRINKING GUITAR
00159517 .... $9.99

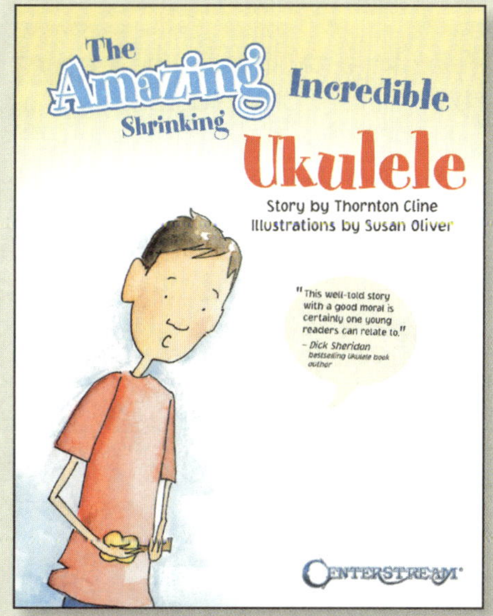

THE AMAZING INCREDIBLE SHRINKING UKULELE
00194560.. $9.99

P.O. Box 17878 - Anaheim Hills, CA 92817

(714) 779-9390 www.centerstream-usa.com

More Great Books from Thornton Cline...

PRACTICE PERSONALITIES: WHAT'S YOUR TYPE?

Identifying and Understanding the Practice Personality Type in the Music Student

by Thornton Cline

Teaching is one of the greatest responsibilities in society. It's an art form that requires craft, patience, creativity, and intelligence. Practice Personalities: What's Your Type? will help teachers, parents and students realize the challenges of practicing, understand the benefits of correct practicing, identify and understand nine practice personality types, and employ useful strategies to effectively motivate and inspire each type of student. The accompanying CD demonstrates effective practice strategies for selected piano, violin and guitar excerpts from the book.

00101974 Book/CD Pack $24.99

Companion DVD Available

00121577 DVD $19.99

PRACTICE PERSONALITIES FOR ADULTS

Identifying and Understanding the Practice Personality Type in the Adult Music Student

by Thornton Cline

Did you know that your personality can affect the way you learn and perform on a musical instrument? This book identifies nine practice personalities in music students. Adults will learn how to practice more effectively and efficiently according to their personalities. A Practice Personalities test is included along with an accompanying CD.

00131613 Book/CD Pack $24.99

P.O. Box 17878 - Anaheim Hills, CA 92817

(714) 779-9390 www.centerstream-usa.com